AF269852

Lerner SPORTS

MEET BRYCE YOUNG

MARGARET J. GOLDSTEIN

Lerner Publications ◆ Minneapolis

Lerner Publications Company
An imprint of Lerner Publishing Group, Inc.
241 First Avenue North
Minneapolis, MN 55401 USA

For reading levels and more information, look up this title at www.lernerbooks.com.

Main body text set in Aptifer Slab LT Pro. Typeface provided by Linotype AG.

Photo Editor: Nicole Berglund

Library of Congress Cataloging-in-Publication Data

Names: Goldstein, Margaret J., author.
Title: Meet Bryce Young : Carolina Panthers superstar / Margaret J. Goldstein.
Description: Minneapolis : Lerner Publications, [2025] | Series: Lerner sports. Sports VIPs | Includes bibliographical references and index. | Audience: Ages 7–11 years | Audience: Grades 2–3 | Summary: "Carolina Panthers quarterback Bryce Young was drafted with the first overall pick in 2023. Discover how Young won the Heisman Trophy in college and his success in the National Football League"— Provided by publisher.
Identifiers: LCCN 2023054851 (print) | LCCN 2023054852 (ebook) | ISBN 9798765626023 (lib. bdg.) | ISBN 9798765629765 (pbk.) | ISBN 9798765637722 (epub)
Subjects: LCSH: Young, Bryce, 2001-—Juvenile literature. | Quarterbacks (Football)—Pennsylvania—Biography—Juvenile literature. | African American football players—Pennsylvania—Biography—Juvenile literature. | Football players—United States—Biography—Juvenile literature. | University of Alabama—Sports—History—Juvenile literature. | Heisman Trophy—History—Juvenile literature. | Carolina Panthers (Football team)—Juvenile literature. | National Football League—Juvenile literature.
Classification: LCC GV939.Y67 G65 2025 (print) | LCC GV939.Y67 (ebook) | DDC 796.332092 [B]—dc23/eng/20240131

LC record available at https://lccn.loc.gov/2023054851
LC ebook record available at https://lccn.loc.gov/2023054852

Manufactured in the United States of America
1-1010135-51936-2/29/2024

TABLE OF CONTENTS

THE REAL DEAL

The University of Alabama trailed Kansas State University 10–0. If quarterback Bryce Young and his Alabama teammates were going to win the 2022 Sugar Bowl, they needed to up their game. At the end of the first quarter, Young took the snap. He scanned the field for an open receiver. He spotted teammate Isaiah Bond in the back of the end zone. Young stepped forward and threw the ball. Touchdown Alabama!

Alabama was on the scoreboard. They didn't hold back. In the next quarter, Young threw a short pass to teammate Cameron Latu for another touchdown. This put Alabama in the lead. Young was on fire as he hit Jermaine Burton for another score. At halftime, Alabama led 21–10.

FAST FACTS

DATE OF BIRTH: July 25, 2001
POSITION: quarterback
LEAGUE: National Football League (NFL)

PROFESSIONAL HIGHLIGHTS: Heisman Trophy winner; number one pick in the NFL draft; 2022 Sugar Bowl champion

PERSONAL HIGHLIGHTS: loves to play basketball; studied psychology; hosted a football podcast in college

Young prepares to throw during the 2022 Sugar Bowl.

In the third quarter, Young struck again. This time, Ja'Corey Brooks caught his pass for a touchdown. Young closed the night with a 47-yard touchdown pass to Kobe Prentice. Alabama went on to win the game 45 to 20.

After the game, Young was named the Sugar Bowl's Most Valuable Player. This was one of many honors he received during his college career, including the 2021 Heisman Trophy. Coaches, reporters, and other players were impressed by his skill. "This guy is the real deal as a quarterback," said NFL analyst Scott Pioli. "This is the guy you want leading your offense and leading your huddle."

The Sugar Bowl was Young's last college football game. He would soon enter the NFL draft. He was ready to compete with the best football players in the world.

Young holds up a trophy after winning the 2022 Sugar Bowl.

CHAPTER 1

WHEN YOUNG WAS YOUNG

Bryce Young was born on July 25, 2001. He grew up near Los Angeles, California. Bryce is the only child of Craig and Julie Young. Craig Young is a mental health therapist, and Julie Young worked for many years as a special education teacher.

Bryce got into football at a young age. His father says that Bryce could catch a cloth football when he was just four months old. By the time Bryce was a toddler, he was already throwing the ball. He organized games with other kids as he got older. Bryce played basketball too. He played at school and with youth sports programs.

Young (*center*) stands with his parents, Craig and Julie, in 2022.

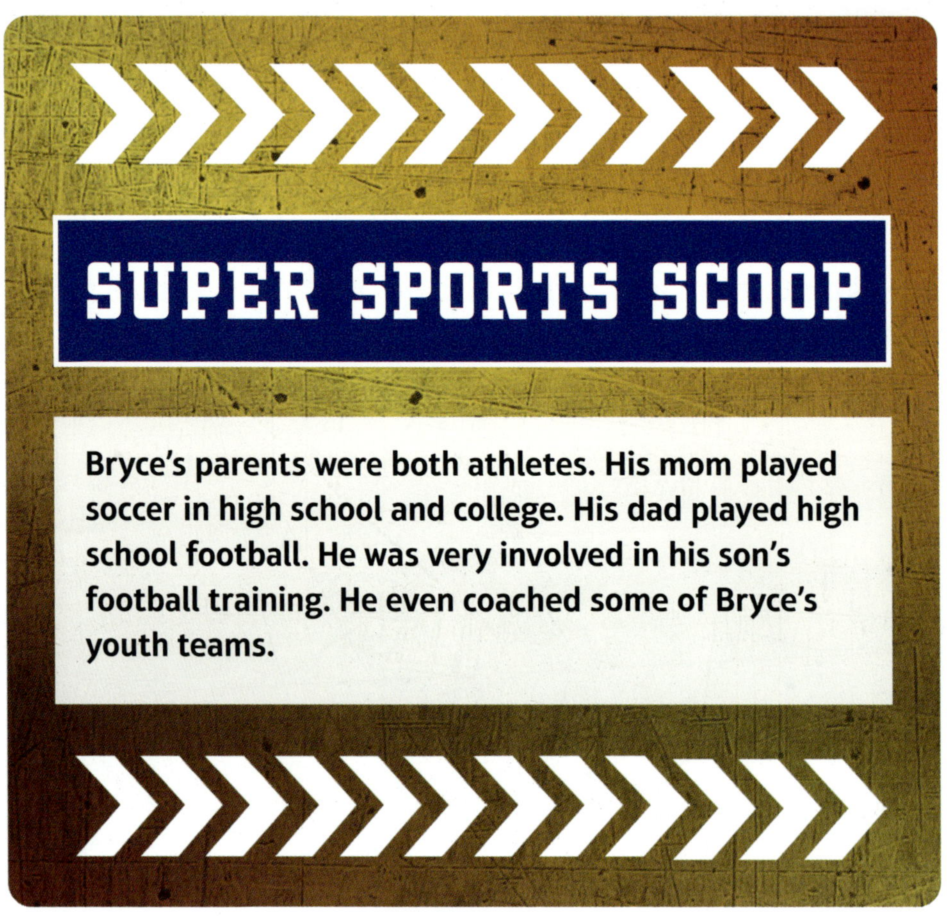

On the basketball court, Bryce was an outstanding point guard. He was a skilled ball handler and shooter. In football, he played quarterback. He was a standout thanks to his agility and quick, accurate passes. Although Bryce excelled at two sports, he decided to put his energy into football. He started to dream big. He thought about playing college football and even joining the NFL one day.

Stephen Curry (*right*) dribbles past a defender in 2024.

SUPER SPORTS SCOOP

Bryce stopped playing organized basketball after high school, but he still enjoyed the sport. He loved watching it on TV. His favorite player was Stephen Curry.

CHAPTER 2

AIMING HIGH

In 2016 Bryce started at Cathedral High School. It is an all-boys school in Los Angeles. In his first year, he was the school's backup quarterback. He took over as starting quarterback as a sophomore. That year he passed for 3,431 yards and threw 41 touchdowns. Cathedral ended the season with a stellar 10–2 record.

Bryce wanted to take his game to the next level. He transferred to Mater Dei High School in Santa Ana, California. Mater Dei has one of the best high school football programs in the country.

Bryce (*left*) runs with the football during a 2018 game with Mater Dei.

Bryce (*left*) sprints down the field in 2018.

The Mater Dei coaches chose Bryce as their starting quarterback. He played like a star. In his junior year, he passed for 3,846 yards and threw 39 touchdowns. Bryce led the Mater Dei Monarchs to victory at the 2018 California state championship.

Bryce posted big numbers again in 2019. This helped his team win. During that season, the team won 13 games and lost only one. Bryce also won many awards that year. He was named the Gatorade High School Football Player of the Year for California and *USA Today*'s High School Offensive Player of the Year.

As a senior, Young passed for 4,528 yards and threw 58 touchdowns.

CHAPTER 3

COLLEGE CHAMP

Major college football teams wanted Young in their lineup. They offered Young scholarships. At first he leaned toward the University of Southern California. But he decided to attend the University of Alabama.

The team had a long list of division and national
championships. They also had famous coaches. Young was
excited to join.

In 2020 Young started his first year at Alabama. In the
classroom, he studied psychology. On the football field,
he played backup quarterback behind starter Mac Jones.

Young (*right*) sprints with the
football during a 2022 game.

Young didn't get much playing time that year. But he was eager to learn from his coaches and teammates. When he did play, he posted good numbers.

After Jones went pro, Young took over as starting quarterback. He immediately hit the ground running. In a November 2021 game against Arkansas, he threw for a total of 559 yards for five touchdowns. It was a new school record.

Young (*left*) rushes past an opponent in 2021.

In the Iron Bowl against Auburn University, Alabama was on the verge of defeat. Young led a 97-yard drive for a touchdown with just 24 seconds left in the game. That score tied the game, and Alabama won it in overtime. Eight days later, Young and his teammates went to the SEC Championships. They faced the nation's number one ranking team, the University of Georgia. Alabama won big, 41–24.

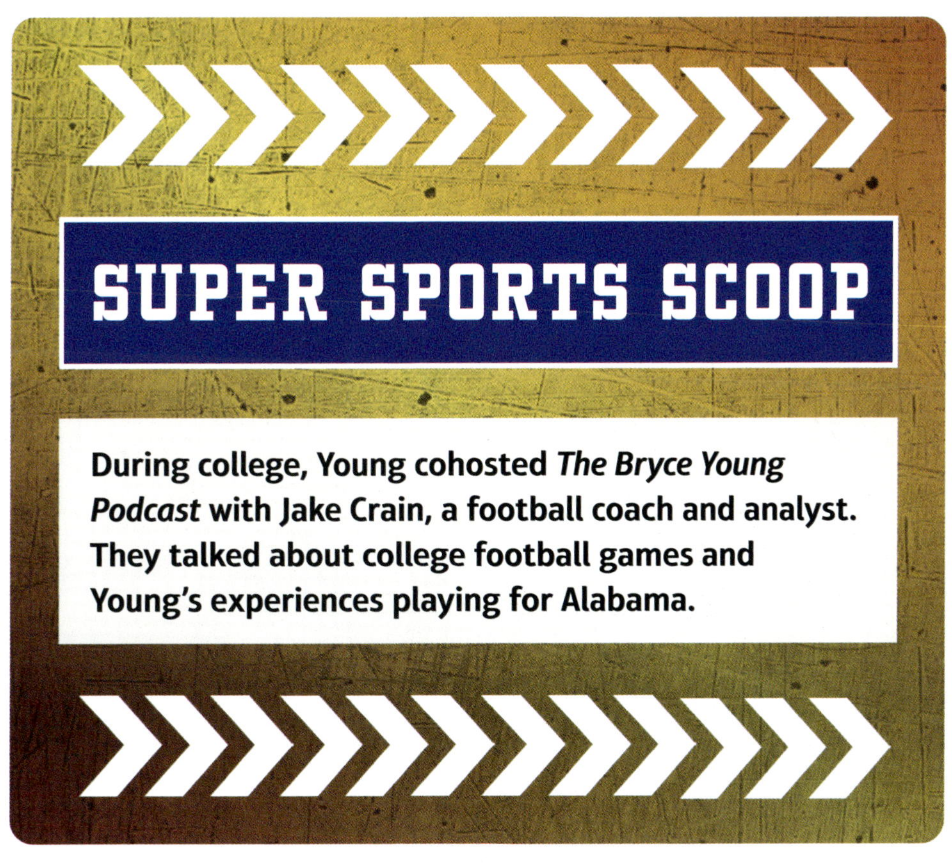

"Bryce is kind of the calm in the midst of chaos,"
said Coach Nick Saban. "I think it comes from his great
preparation. He's really confident, he has a presence
about him. He impacts the players around him in a very
positive way."

Will Anderson Jr., an Alabama defensive end, called
Young "very smart, very instinctive." Anderson added,
"He can make plays even in the toughest situations. He
can get away from being sacked . . . He comes to work
hard, he never slacks."

Young (*right*) and Nick Saban celebrate a 2021 win.

Young holds the Heisman Trophy in 2021.

At the end of the 2021 season, Young won many of college football's top honors. He received the Associated Press Player of the Year award, the Maxwell Award for best player, and the Davey O'Brien National Quarterback Award. He also won the oldest, grandest honor of all, the Heisman Trophy, given to college football's most outstanding player. Young was humble when he accepted the award. He stated that he couldn't have succeeded without his teammates. He thanked his family and coaches for believing in him and guiding him.

CHAPTER 4

DRAFTED

As a junior, Young continued to amaze football fans. In 2022, the team went 11–2 and won the Sugar Bowl. Young threw for 3,328 yards and 32 touchdowns that season.

Players who have finished three years of college can choose to skip their fourth year and enter the NFL draft. Young felt he was ready for the pros and joined the draft. On draft day, Young sat with his family at Union Station in Kansas City, Missouri. NFL commissioner Roger Goodell walked onto the stage and announced the first pick: Bryce Young! Young was headed to the Carolina Panthers.

Young smiles with his jersey after being chosen by the Carolina Panthers in 2023.

Young moved to Charlotte, North Carolina, which is the Panthers' home base. He spent most of his summer at their training camp, preparing for his pro debut. The Panthers had endured a string of losing seasons in prior years. They hoped to rebuild their team with Young as the centerpiece. But in the fall of 2023, he and the Panthers struggled. In college, Young had been a strong passer. But with Carolina, he threw poorly. Many of his passes were incomplete. By the end of the season, Carolina had lost 15 games and won only two.

Panthers fans were disappointed in Young. But many stressed that a quarterback can't win on his own. They said Young needed a better offensive line to protect him. He needed skilled receivers to catch the ball. He needed a stronger defensive line to keep opponents from scoring.

Young (*center*) talks with Carolina's offensive line during a 2023 game.

Young took responsibility for his mistakes. He also encouraged his teammates to turn their disappointment into something positive. "Being frustrated, it's not going to win a game and not going to help," he said. "You have to turn that [energy] and use that in action throughout the week, and then we have to translate it [into game day]."

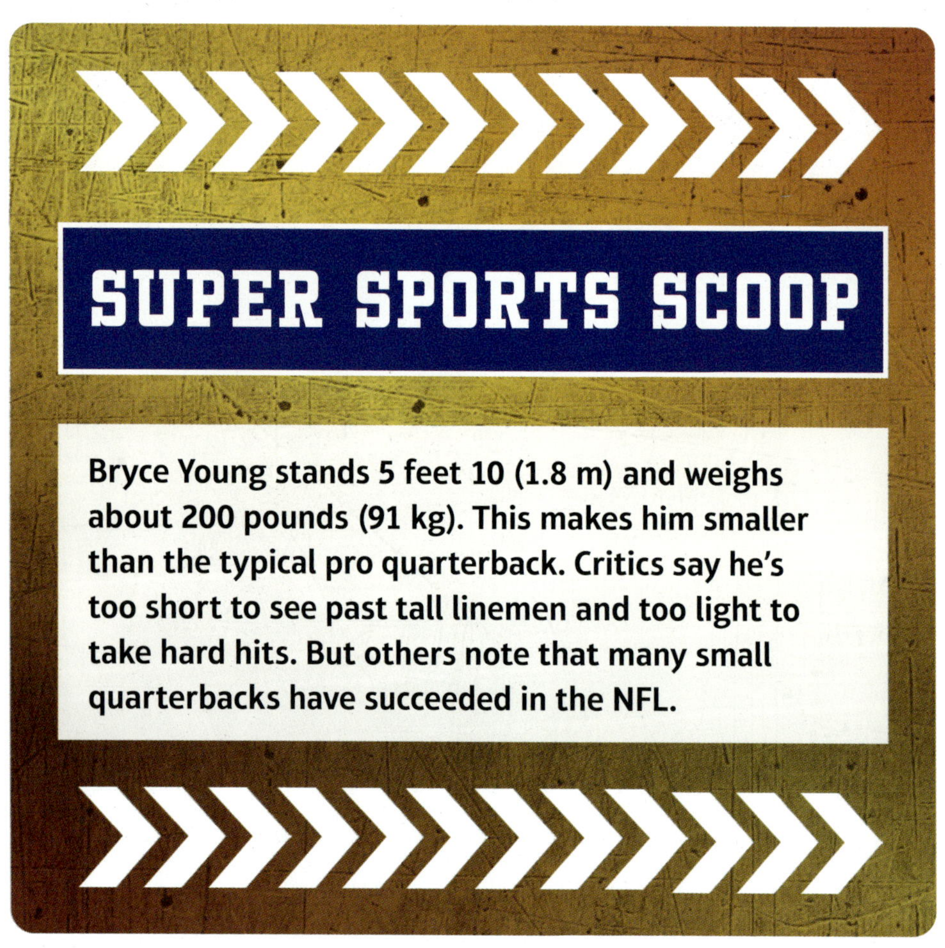

Win or lose, Young strongly believes in himself. As he said when he accepted the Heisman Trophy, "People, a lot of times, have told me that I wasn't going to be able to make it. And for me, it's always been about not really proving them wrong, but proving to myself what I can accomplish. I always push myself to work the hardest, and try my best to do all I can to maximize all I can do."

Bryce Young is just getting started in the toughest football league. If he keeps pushing himself, there's no limit to what he can do.

BRYCE YOUNG CAREER STATS

GAMES STARTED:
16

PASSES ATTEMPTED:
527

PASSES COMPLETED:
315

PASSING TOUCHDOWNS:
11

PASSING YARDS:
2,877

INTERCEPTIONS:
10

*Statistics are accurate through the 2023 regular NFL season.

GLOSSARY

analyst: a person who studies something

draft: a system for choosing new players to join a professional sports league

huddle: a brief on-field meeting where players discuss the next play

incomplete: a football pass that is not caught

linemen: players positioned near the line of scrimmage, where the offense and defense meet at the start of a play

point guard: a basketball player who focuses on setting up plays and passing the ball to scorers

psychology: the scientific study of the human mind

receiver: a player who catches passes thrown by the quarterback

sack: to tackle a quarterback behind the line of scrimmage, before they can throw or hand off the football

scholarship: money granted to pay for a student's education

SOURCE NOTES

7 "Top QB Prospect Bryce Young, C.J. Stroud Measure Up at Combine," Field Level Media, March 3, 2023, https:// fieldlevelmedia.com/latest-sports-news/top-qb-prospects -bryce-young-c-j-stroud-measure-up-at-combine-2/.

20 Tony Tsoukalas, "Alabama Quarterback Bryce Young Wins Heisman Trophy," Tide Illustrated, December 11, 2021, https:// alabama.rivals.com/news/alabama-quarterback-bryce -young-wins-heisman-trophy.

20 Tsoukalas.

26 David Newton, "Panthers, Bryce Young 'Frustrated' by Loss to Bears," ABC11, November 10, 2023, https://abc11.com/sports /panthers-bryce-young-frustrated-by-loss-to-bears/14039803/.

27 Nick Gray, "What Alabama Football QB Bryce Young Said in Speech after Winning Heisman Trophy," *Tuscaloosa (AL) News*, December 11, 2021, https://www.tuscaloosanews.com/story /sports/2021/12/11/bryce-young-alabama-football-heisman -trophy-speech-acceptance/6481205001/.

LEARN MORE

Britannica Kids: Football

https://kids.britannica.com/students/article/football/274377

Coleman, Ted. *Carolina Panthers: All-Time Greats*. Mendota Heights, MN: Press Box Books, 2022.

Ducksters: National Football League

https://www.ducksters.com/sports/national_football_league.php

Kiddle: College Football Facts for Kids

https://kids.kiddle.co/College_football

Lowe, Alexander. *G.O.A.T. Football Quarterbacks*. Minneapolis: Lerner Publications, 2023.

Meier, William. *Alabama Crimson Tide*. Minneapolis: SportsZone, 2021.

INDEX

PHOTO ACKNOWLEDGMENTS

Image credits: AP Photo/Brian Westerholt, p. 4; AP Photo/Butch Dill, pp. 6–8, 17; Jonathan Mailhes/Cal Sport Media/Alamy, p. 9; AP Photo/Brandon Dill, p. 11; AP Photo/Kirby Lee, p. 12; AP Photo/Louis Lopez/Cal Sport Media, pp. 13–15; AP Photo/Vasha Hunt, pp. 16, 18; AP Photo/Logan Bowles, p. 20; AP Photo/Rich Graessle/Icon Sportswire, p. 21; AP Photo/Erik Verduzco, p. 22; AP Photo/Chris Carlson, p. 23; Jacob Kupferman/Stringer/Getty Images, p. 24; AP Photo/Phelan M. Ebenhack, p. 25; AP Photo/Doug Murray, p. 27.

Cover: AP Photo/Margaret Bowles.